HOMAGE TO

CHICHEN ITZA

New Wonder of the World

INDEX

Presentation · 5

Map of the site · 6

Temple of the Warriors · 8

The Castle or Pyramid of Kukulcan · 9

The Castle or Pyramid of Kukulcan · 10

Ball Court · 11

Temple of the Warriors · 12

The Church · 13

The Snail or Observatory · 14-15

Chichanchob · 16

Temple of the Warriors · 17

The Snail or Observatory · 18

Ball Court · 19

Platform of Venus · 20

Temple of the Warriors · 21

East Annex of the Nunnery and the Church · 22-23

Substructure of the Castle · 24

Acetate: equinox · 25

The Castle or Pyramid of Kukulcan · 26

Annex to the Temple of Jaguars · 27

Temple of the Warriors · 28

East Annex of the Nunnery · 29

Ball Court · 30-31

Temple of the Warriors · 32

The Sacred Cenote · 33

Plaza of the Thousand Columns · 34

The Snail or Observatory · 35

Platform of Eagles and Jaguars · 36

House of Shells · 37

Ball Court · 38-39

The Castle or Pyramid of Kukulcan · 40

Temple of the Phalluses · 41

Platform of Venus · 42

Temple of the Owls · 43

The Castle or Pyramid of Kukulcan · 44

Tzompantli · 45

Temple of the Warriors · 46-47

PRESENTATION

Chichen Itza, chosen as a Wonder of the Modern World, was one of the most highly developed cities of Mayan civilization. Its impressive buildings still stand as witnesses to its greatness.

The Pyramid of Kukulcan is one of the tallest and most remarkable buildings in the canon of Mayan architecture. It must have been constructed during the peak of Itzá-Cocóm culture. In the interior is another pyramid-sanctuary, built many years before, which Mayan architects covered over as a foundation for the new structure.

Today, the entrance to the archaeological zone leads to the so-called Great Level, a wide grass-covered expanse where several of the most imposing buildings of the ancient city stand.

Page 2: View of the Castle from the Temple of the Warriors.
Previous page: The Castle or Pyramid of Kukulcan.

MAP OF THE SITE

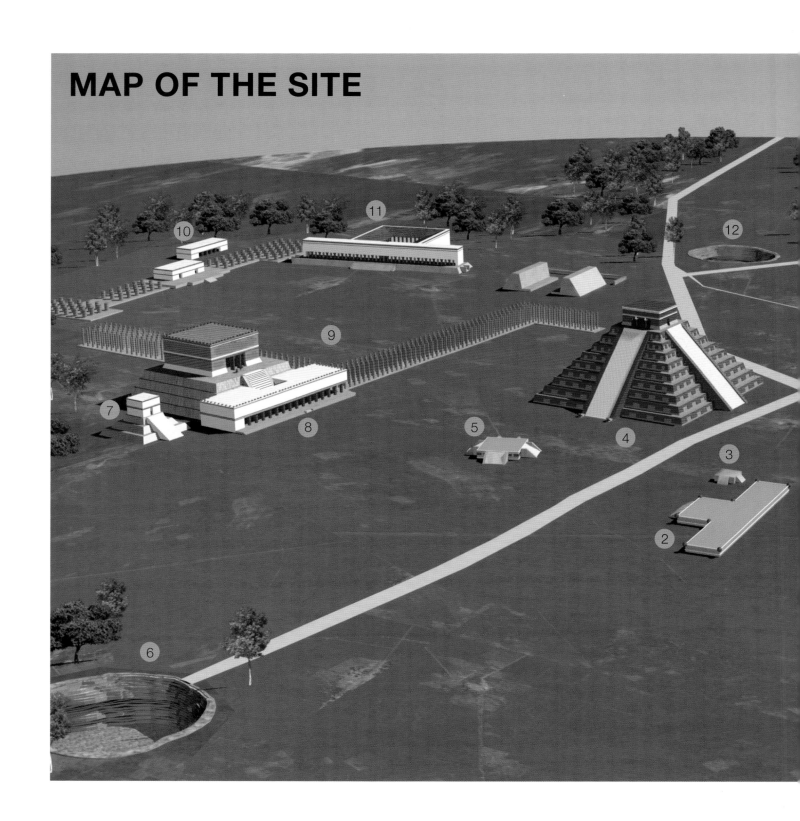

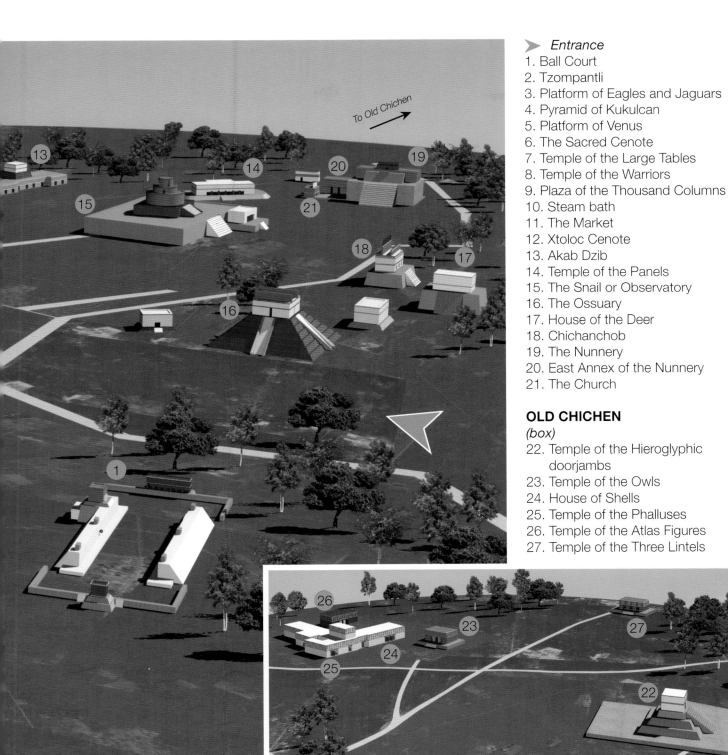

To Old Chichen →

➤ *Entrance*
1. Ball Court
2. Tzompantli
3. Platform of Eagles and Jaguars
4. Pyramid of Kukulcan
5. Platform of Venus
6. The Sacred Cenote
7. Temple of the Large Tables
8. Temple of the Warriors
9. Plaza of the Thousand Columns
10. Steam bath
11. The Market
12. Xtoloc Cenote
13. Akab Dzib
14. Temple of the Panels
15. The Snail or Observatory
16. The Ossuary
17. House of the Deer
18. Chichanchob
19. The Nunnery
20. East Annex of the Nunnery
21. The Church

OLD CHICHEN
(box)
22. Temple of the Hieroglyphic doorjambs
23. Temple of the Owls
24. House of Shells
25. Temple of the Phalluses
26. Temple of the Atlas Figures
27. Temple of the Three Lintels

Above: Long-nosed Chaac mask.
Following page: South façade of the Pyramid of Kukulcan.

Previous page: Serpents' heads at the base of the Castle.
Above: Temple of the Jaguars and wall of the Ball Court.

Above: Chac Mool flanked by pilasters in the shape of serpents.
Following page: Chaac mask.

Previous page: Panorama of the Snail or Observatory.
Above: The Chichanchob or Red House.
Following page: Backlit Mask in the Temple of the Warriors.

16

Previous page: Detail of the Observatory Tower.
Above: Stone ring from the Ball Court.

19

Above: Bas-relief of the planet Venus.
Following page: Backlit serpentine columns.
Following double page: East Annex of the Nunnery and the Church.

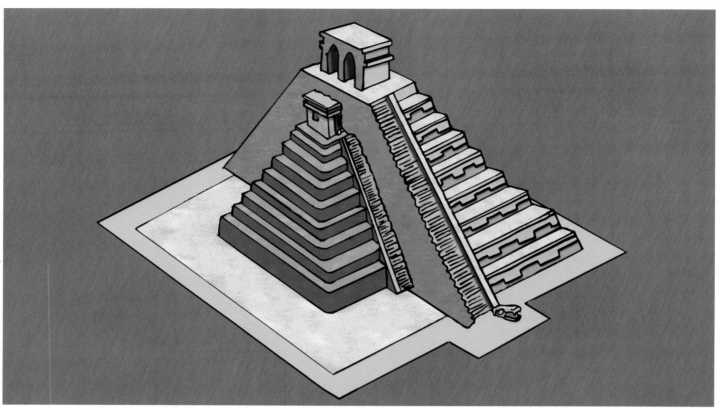

Above: Section of the Pyramid of Kukulcan and the Substructure.
Below: Jaguar throne and Chac Mool found in the chambers of the Substructure.
Following page: Representation of the Equinox.

Previous page: North façade of the Castle.
Above: Jaguar throne in the Annex to the Temple of Jaguars.

Above: Kukulcan emerging from the jaws of a plumed serpent.
Following page: Detail of the East Annex to the Nunnery.

Previous page: Panorama of the Ball Court.
Above: Detail of the serpentine columns in the Temple of the Warriors.
Following page: The Sacred Cenote.

Previous page: Plaza of the Thousand Columns.
Above: The Snail or Observatory.

Above: Detail of the Platform of Eagles and Jaguars.
Following page: Detail of a column in the shape of an Atlas in the House of Shells.

Previous page: South Temple of the Ball Court.
Above: View of the Castle from the Temple of Warriors.
Following page: Detail of the frieze on the Temple of the Phalluses.

Previous page: Detail of the Platform of Venus.
Above: Mask on the Temple of the Owls.

Above: Main façade of the Castle.
Following page: Detail of the Tzompantli.
Following double page: Temple of the Warriors.

HOMAGE TO **CHICHEN ITZA**
New Wonder of the World
1st edition, 2008

ISBN 970-605-360-3

All Rights Reserved © Editorial Dante S.A. de C.V.
Calle 17 No. 138-B por Prolongación Paseo de Montejo
C.P. 97100. Mérida, Yucatán, México.

Editor in chief • Hervé Baeza Braga
Creative control • Laura Morales Encalada
Photographs • David Baeza Braga
Digital retouching of photographs and
the representation of the equinox • Laura Morales
Map illustration • Laura Reyes Pascual
Translation • David Phillips

PRINTED IN CHINA